MACDONALD STARTERS

Dogs

Macdonald Educational

About Macdonald Starters

Macdonald Starters are vocabulary controlled information books for young children. More than ninety per cent of the words in the text will be in the reading vocabulary of the vast majority of young readers. Word and sentence length have also been carefully controlled.

Key new words associated with the topic of each book are repeated with picture explanations in the Starters dictionary at the end. The dictionary can also be used as an index for teaching children to look things up.

Teachers and experts have been consulted on the content and accuracy of the books.

Illustrated by: Tony Herbert

Editors: Peter Usborne, Su Swallow, Jennifer Vaughan

Reading consultant: Donald Moyle, author of *The Teaching of Reading* and senior lecturer in education at Edge Hill College of Education

Chairman, teacher advisory panel: F. F. Blackwell, general inspector for schools, London Borough of Croydon, with responsibility for primary education

Teacher panel: Elizabeth Wray, Loveday Harmer, Lynda Snowdon, Joy West

ISBN 0 356 03841 6
First published 1971 by Macdonald Educational
St Giles House
49–50 Poland Street
London W1

This is our dog.
She is very fat.
She is going to have some puppies.

1

She has six puppies.
She gives them milk.
2

At first the puppies cannot see.
They cannot walk.

After ten days the puppies can see.
Soon they can walk too.

4

Now the puppies are six weeks old.
They can eat from a dish.
They can eat meat and drink water.

This dog is one year old.
He is grown up now.
He loves to run.
He must not run on the road.

6

Some dogs like being brushed.
Brushing is good for dogs.
Sometimes a dog must have a bath.

7

Dogs can make a lot of noise.
They bark.
Sometimes dogs growl too.
8

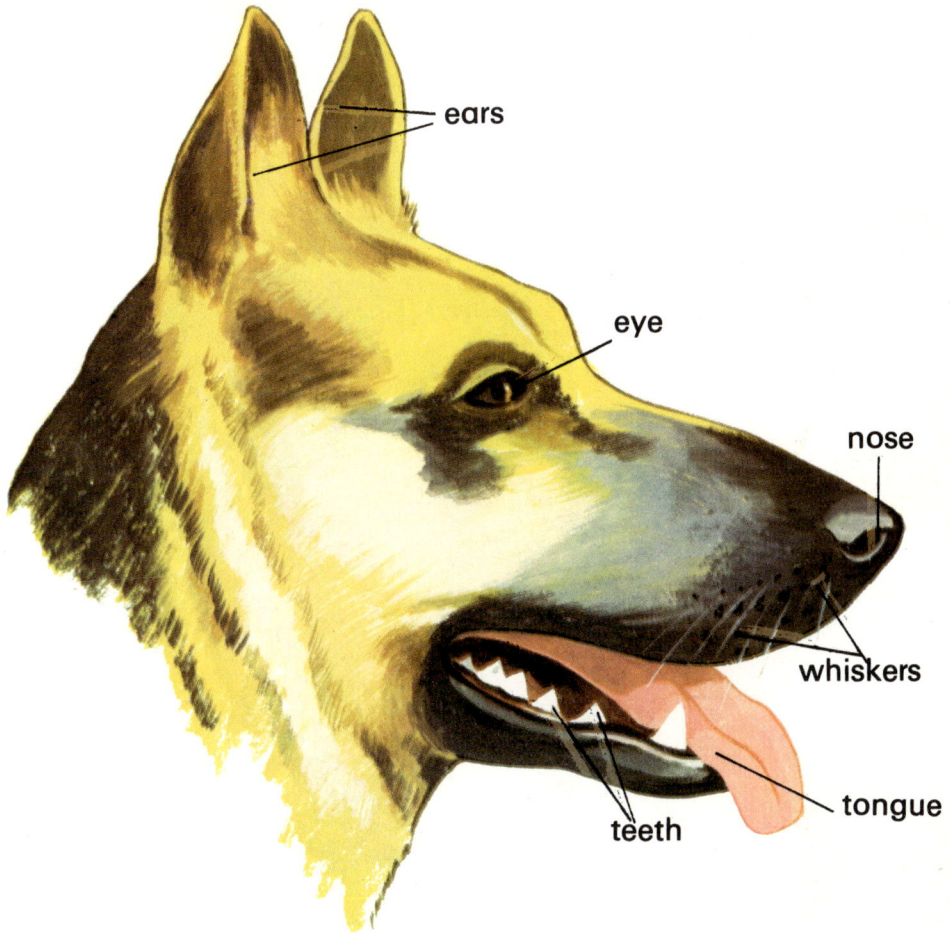

ears

eye

nose

whiskers

tongue

teeth

Dogs have sharp teeth.
They have good noses to smell with.
Good teeth and noses
help dogs to hunt.

This dog can smell a rat.
He hunts for the rat.
10

This is a wild dog.
Wild dogs must hunt for their food.

Some kinds of wild dogs
hunt in packs.

12

There are packs of tame dogs too.
Eskimos keep packs of huskies.
Huskies pull sledges.

13

Farmers often keep sheepdogs.
A sheepdog rounds up the sheep.
He brings them to the farm.
14

A sheep is lost in the snow.
A sheepdog is helping to find it.

This is a police dog.
He is helping the policeman
to catch a robber.

16

This man cannot see.
He is blind.
His dog helps him find his way.

Long ago a queen kept a little dog.
She kept him in her sleeve.

A king once kept dogs like this.
They were long-haired greyhounds.
The king kept them for hunting.

Many other people kept
big dogs for hunting.

Long ago knights kept dogs.
Sometimes knights slept in tents.
The dogs looked after the knights.

fox

wolf

coyote

dingo

These animals are all like dogs.
They are in the dog family.

Starter's **Dogs** words

puppy
(page 1)

teeth
(page 9)

dish
(page 5)

tongue
(page 9)

road
(page 6)

nose
(page 9)

brush
(page 7)

rat
(page 10)

bath
(page 7)

pack
(page 12)

Eskimo
(page 13)

sheep
(page 14)

husky
(page 13)

farm
(page 14)

sleigh
(page 13)

police dog
(page 16)

farmer
(page 14)

policeman
(page 16)

sheep dog
(page 14)

queen
(page 18)

sleeve
(page 18)

fox
(page 22)

greyhound
(page 19)

wolf
(page 22)

knight
(page 21)

coyote
(page 22)

tent
(page 21)

dingo
(page 22)